RONALDO CHOPS AND JERSEY SWAPS

SOCCER'S MOST SIGNATURE
MOVES, CELEBRATIONS, AND MORE

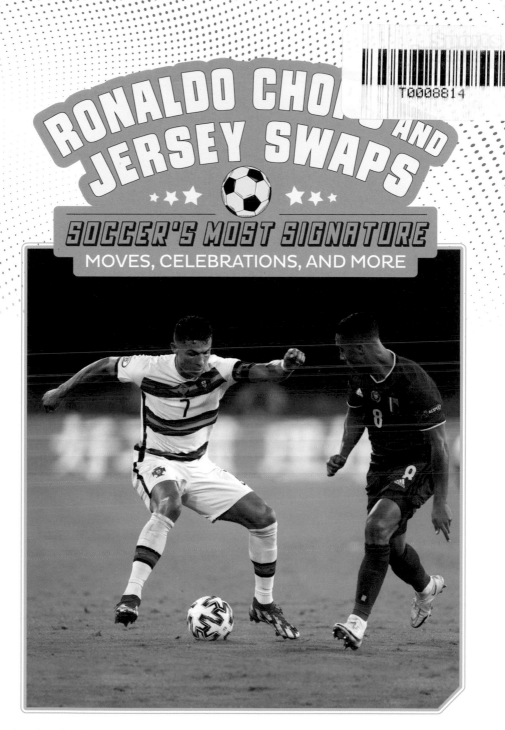

by Steve Foxe

CAPSTONE PRESS
a capstone imprint

T0008814

Published by Capstone Press, an imprint of Capstone
1710 Roe Crest Drive, North Mankato, Minnesota 56003
capstonepub.com

Library of Congress Cataloging-in-Publication Data is available on the
Library of Congress website.

ISBN: 9781669065548 (hardcover)
ISBN: 9781669065494 (paperback)
ISBN: 9781669065500 (ebook PDF)

Summary: Megan Rapinoe's statue pose. Pelé's rabona kick. The Ronaldo chop.
These are some of soccer's most signature moves and celebrations! In this high-
interest book, discover the history behind these iconic moves and many more—
from the athletes who made them famous to their history within the game.

Editorial Credits
Editor: Donald Lemke; Designer: Kayla Rossow; Media Researcher:
Svetlana Zhurkin; Production Specialist: Katy LaVigne

Image Credits
Associated Press: Pool/Thanassis Stavrakis, cover, 1; Getty Images:
AFP/Franck Fife, 21, AFP/Lionel Bonaventure, 23, Dan Istitene, 9, Denis Doyle,
14, 17, Elsa, 5, Gonzalo Arroyo Moreno, 16, Jed Jacobsohn, 25, Juan Manuel
Serrano Arce, 15, Julian Finney, 4 (bottom), Keystone, 11, Rick Stewart, 19,
Valerio Pennicino, 18; Newscom: Action Plus/John Patrick Fletcher, 13, Mirrorpix/
John Varley, 29; Shutterstock: Alexander_P, 8 and throughout, Alexey Seleykov
(soccer ball), cover, 1, DarkPlatypus (dotted wave), back cover and throughout,
GelgelNasution (soccer player), 4 (top) and throughout; Sports Illustrated: Jerry
Cooke, 7, Robert Beck, 26, 27

All internet sites appearing in back matter were available and accurate when this
book was sent to press.

TABLE OF CONTENTS

Words in **bold** are in the glossary.

SIGNATURE SOCCER

Soccer is a sport enjoyed around the world. It is filled with dazzling kicks, last-minute goals, and thrilling wins.

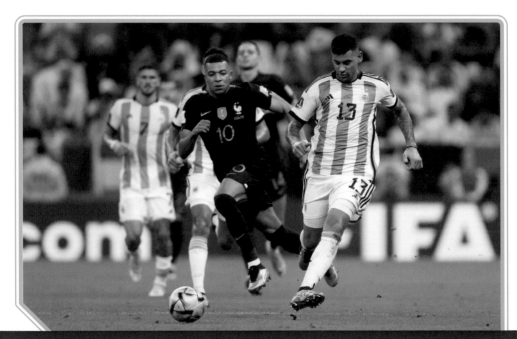

Players for Argentina and France compete during the 2022 FIFA World Cup.

Megan Rapinoe celebrates after scoring a goal.

Some soccer moves and celebrations are extra special. They're one-of-a-kind, fan-**famous**, or impossible to stop. They are often called soccer's most **signature** moves.

PLAYING HOOKY

Edson Arantes do Nascimento, better known as Pelé, is often called the greatest soccer player of all time. The International Olympic Committee named him Athlete of the Century in 1999. Early in his career, Pelé helped turn a simple kick into one of the game's most signature moves.

Pelé won his first World Cup at the age of 17 when he played for Brazil in 1958.

Pelé playing for the New York Cosmos in 1975

The kick that Pelé made famous is called the **rabona**. This name comes from a Spanish word meaning "playing hooky."

To perform the kick, a player plants one foot close to the ball. They swing their other leg behind their planted leg. Then, the player kicks the ball with their legs crossed!

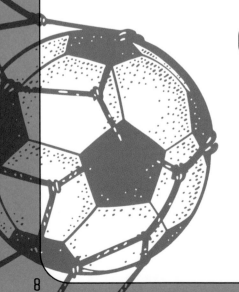

PELÉ'S WORLD CUP STATS

Games Played: 14
Goals: 12
Championships:

Barcelona's Neymar Júnior (right) performs a rabona kick.

Pelé didn't create the rabona kick. But he was one of the first players to have it recorded on video. After seeing Pelé do it, more players started using this unique kick.

TURN IT UP!

Dutch sports hero Johan Cruyff is one of soccer's all-time legends. After he stopped playing, Cruyff became a successful coach and manager in the sport as well.

Cruyff played for the Netherlands national team and helped them reach the World Cup final in 1974.

Johan Cruyff plays against Uruguay in 1974.

During his playing days, Cruyff perfected a move that still carries his name. It is known as the "Cruyff turn."

Cruyff knew that one of the most important skills of soccer is keeping control of the ball. The Cruyff turn allows a player to completely change direction if the other team has them blocked.

With one leg beside the ball, Cruyff would use the other to kick the ball straight behind him. Cruyff would then turn around sharply to drive the ball back and around the opposing team.

An Arsenal Football Club player performs a Cruyff turn.

GET THE CHOP

Portugal's Cristiano Ronaldo has won dozens of trophies. He has been given the European Golden Shoe award four times.

That's more than any other player in Europe! When Ronaldo scores a goal, he often jumps and shouts, "Siiiuuu!" It's his signature celebration.

But there's another move that's named after him: the "Ronaldo chop."

To perform his famous chop, Ronaldo leaps in front of the ball. He kicks it at an angle using the inside of his strong foot.

Ronaldo prepares to chop the ball with the inside of his right foot.

This helps him change direction quickly.
It confuses the other team. Ronaldo uses
his other foot to protect the ball from being
taken away.

FAKE OUT!

The Elastico is another signature soccer move—and a **tricky** one. The move was made famous by two-time FIFA World Player of the Year Ronaldinho.

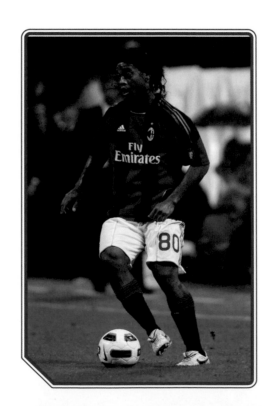

The move involves kicking the ball away using the outside of the shoe and then quickly kicking it back with the inside of the shoe. It can fool defenders and help with dribbling. It's a strong move on the pitch!

STRIKE A POSE

American Megan Rapinoe is one of the most awarded women in soccer. In 2019, she also gave the sport one of its biggest viral moments.

After scoring two goals against France in the Women's World Cup quarter-final match, Rapinoe **posed** with her arms up and a grin on her face.

Megan Rapinoe poses at the 2019 Women's World Cup.

Photos of this victory pose quickly spread across social media. It inspired **memes** and many comments.

Rapinoe is known for her **confidence** on and off the field. It's no surprise that photos of the pose took off!

SHIRTS VS. SKINS

It's common for male players to rip off their jerseys in celebration of scoring a goal or winning a game. But in 1999, U.S. women's soccer player Brandi Chastain caused a stir when she did the same.

After scoring a penalty kick against China in the final round of the Women's World Cup, Chastain took off her shirt. She spun it around her head before dropping to her knees. Some people believed it was wrong for a woman soccer player to celebrate this way. Others loved it!

Sports Illustrated featured Chastain on the cover in July 1999.

Chastain stood by her decision. The photos of her celebrating her winning goal ended up on the covers of *Newsweek*, *Time Magazine*, and *Sports Illustrated*. They inspired girls around the world.

A DIFFERENT KIND OF TROPHY

One of the greatest signs of respect between athletes is swapping jerseys after a game. Although taking someone else's sweaty clothes may sound gross, it's a way to remember a hard-fought game.

The tradition is at least a century old in soccer. One of the most memorable jersey swaps was in 1970. Soccer legends Pelé and Bobby Moore swapped jerseys after their teams, Brazil and England, faced each other in the World Cup.

Pelé and Moore swap jerseys at the World Cup in 1970.

GLOSSARY

confidence (KON-fih-dehns)— a feeling of certainty

famous (FAY-mus)—well-known or widely recognized

meme (MEEM)— a funny or interesting picture or video that is spread widely online especially through social media

pose (POHZ)—to strike a specific stance or position, usually to celebrate or express confidence

rabona (ruh-BOH-nuh)—a soccer kick where a player swings their stronger foot from behind their other leg to strike the ball with the outside of their shoe

signature (SIG-nuh-chur)—a distinctive or unique mark, move, or style that represents someone

tricky (TRIK-ee)—difficult to do or understand, often involving cleverness or deception

READ MORE

Berglund, Bruce. *Big-Time Soccer Records.* North Mankato, MN: Capstone, 2021.

Troupe, Thomas Kingsley. *Strikers and Scarves: Behind the Scenes of Match Day Soccer.* North Mankato, MN: Capstone, 2023.

Scheff, Matt. *Teamwork on the Soccer Field: And Other Soccer Skills.* North Mankato, MN: Capstone, 2022.

INTERNET SITES

National Soccer Hall of Fame
nationalsoccerhof.com

Sports Illustrated Kids
sikids.com

U.S. Soccer
ussoccer.com

INDEX

ABOUT THE AUTHOR

Steve Foxe is the Eisner and Ringo Award-nominated author of over 75 comics and children's books including *X-Men '92: House of XCII*, *Rainbow Bridge*, *Adventure Kingdom,* and the Spider-Ham series from Scholastic. He has written for properties like Pokémon, Mario, LEGO City, Batman, Justice League, Baby Shark, and many more.